Letting Go

Prayers for those
facing the end of a
relationship

Illustrated by Lyn Ellis

Kevin Mayhew

First published in Great Britain in 1994 by
KEVIN MAYHEW LTD
Rattlesden
Bury St Edmunds
Suffolk IP30 0SZ

ISBN 0 86209 450 X

© 1994 Kevin Mayhew Limited

Printed in Hong Kong

Contents

	Page
A Token Of Friendship	5
Have mercy	6
Loving Care	7
A Blessing	8
Be at Peace	9
The Lord our Protector	10
Christ Be With Me	11
The Gate of the Year	12
The Lord's Prayer	13
A Prayer for Patience	14
Christ is the Bridge	15
New Life	16
I Said a Prayer	18
I Am With You Always	19
When Dreams Are Broken	20
Paul's Farewell	21

Wings of Faith	22
When You're Lonely	23
The Twenty-Third Psalm	24
A Prayer for Those Who Live Alone	26
God is the Answer	28
From the Lord of Love	30
Beyond the Shadows	32
Since we have been justified	33
You Are There	34
God Has Not Promised	35
Deep Peace	36
Keep me safe	37
Change	38
True Contentment	39
A Prayer When Distracted	40
My God, My God	42
Remind Me, Lord	43
Wholeness	44
I am convinced	46
Hold My Hand	47
The Lord is a refuge	48

A Token Of Friendship

I can't change what you're going through, I have no words to make a difference, no answers or solutions to make things easier for you. But if it helps in any way I want to say I care. Please know that even when you're lonely you're not alone. I'll be here, supporting you with all my thoughts, cheering for you with all my strength, praying for you with all my heart. For whatever you need, for as long as it takes – Lean on my love.

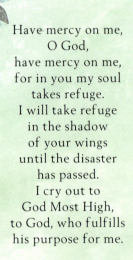

Have mercy on me,
O God,
have mercy on me,
for in you my soul
takes refuge.
I will take refuge
in the shadow
of your wings
until the disaster
has passed.
I cry out to
God Most High,
to God, who fulfills
his purpose for me.

PSALM 57:1-2

LOVING CARE

May God,
who understands each need,
who listens to every prayer,
bless you and keep you
in his loving, tender care.

A Blessing

May the Lord bless you
and take care of you;

May the Lord be kind
and gracious to you;

May the Lord look on you
with favour
and give you peace.

Be at Peace

Do not look forward
to what might happen tomorrow;
the same everlasting Father
who cares for you today
will take care of you
tomorrow and every day.
Be at peace, then, and put aside
all anxious thoughts
and imaginings.

The Lord Our Protector

I lift up my eyes to the hills.
From whence does my help come?
My help comes from the Lord,
who made heaven and earth.

He will not let your foot be moved,
he who keeps you will not slumber.
Behold, he who keeps Israel
will neither slumber nor sleep.

The Lord is your keeper; the Lord
is your shade on your right hand.
The sun shall not smite you by day,
nor the moon by night. The Lord
will keep you from all evil;
he will keep your life. The Lord
will keep your going out
and your coming in,
from this time forth
and for
evermore.

Christ Be With Me

Christ be with me,
Christ within me,
Christ behind me,
Christ before me,
Christ beside me,
Christ to win me,
Christ to comfort
and restore me,

Christ beneath me,
Christ above me,
Christ in quiet,
Christ in danger,
Christ in hearts
of all that love me,
Christ in mouth
of friend and stranger.

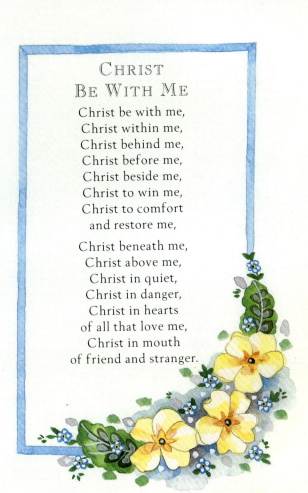

The Gate of the Year

I said to the man
who stood at
the gate of the year
'Give me a light
that I may tread
safely into the unknown.'

And he replied –
'Go out into
the darkness and put your hand
into the hand of God.
That shall be to you better than light
and safer than a known way!'

So I went forth and finding the
hand of God, trod gladly
into the night.

The Lord's Prayer

Our Father,
who art in heaven,
hallowed be thy name.
Thy kingdom come,
thy will be done
on earth as it is in heaven.

Give us this day our daily bread;
and forgive us our trespasses,
as we forgive those who
trespass against us.

And lead us not into temptation,
but deliver us from evil.
For thine is the Kingdom,
the Power and the Glory,
for ever and ever.

A Prayer for Patience

When my patience seems too short
help me stretch it;
teach me how to meet a crisis
with a smile.
When I'm running out of quick
and clever answers
let the questions stop
for just a little while.
When it seems as though
the day has too few hours
in which to do the things
I have to do, may I always find
the time for what's important –
time for listening,
time for love
and laughter
too.

CHRIST IS THE BRIDGE

Christ is the bridge that reaches past today and destiny, to join the things of heaven with those of earth. He links creation's dawning with infinity's vast shore. The arch across all history is his birth. His cross of love is raised above a world where war and sin have torn God and his children far apart. It spans the centuries to give safe passage to his peace.

Christ is the bridge, the way to God's own heart.

NEW LIFE

I had a partner:
now I'm alone.
I feel wronged;
I feel angry;
I feel many things.
Let me be honest,
with you if no one else.

But I don't want to be bitter:
I don't want to nurse a grudge.
I want to be positive;
I want to forgive.
That's hard,
like wood and nails.
It's painful,
like thorns.
I don't know whether I can do it.

But I want life:
new life,
not more of the old.
I know we can't go back.
If there must be a 'death',
before there can be a 'resurrection',
let it be a good death;
without bitterness,
without recrimination.
Let the past be complete.
Let it be buried.

Let the future begin.
For everybody.

MICHAEL FORSTER

I Said a Prayer

I said a prayer for you today
and know God must have heard –
I felt the answer in my heart
although he spoke no word!
I didn't ask for wealth or fame
(I knew you wouldn't mind) –
I asked him to send treasures
of a far more lasting kind!

I asked that he'd be near you
at the start of each new day
to grant you health and blessings
and friends to share your way!
I asked for happiness for you
in all things great and small –
but it was for his loving care
I prayed the most of all!

I Am With You Always

In the springtime
of your life,
when joy is new,
and when the summer
brings the fullness
of your faith, I'm there with you.
I am with you in the autumn
of your years to turn to gold
every memory of your yesterdays,
to banish winter's cold.
I am with you in the sunshine,
when your world glows
warm and bright.
I am with you when life's shadows
bring long hours of endless night.
I am with you every moment,
every hour of every day.
Go in peace upon life's journey,
for I'm with you all the way.

WHEN DREAMS ARE BROKEN

When dreams are broken things
and joy has fled,
there is Jesus.
When hope is a struggle
and faith a fragile thread,
there is Jesus.

When grief is a shadow
and peace unknown,
there is Jesus.
When we need the assurance
that we're not alone,
there is Jesus.

Paul's Farewell

Be happy
and grow in Christ.

Do what I have said,
and live in harmony
and peace.

May the grace of our Lord
Jesus Christ
be with you all.

May God's love,
and the Holy Spirit's
friendship,
be yours.

Wings of Faith

Give us, Lord,
a special faith,
unlimited and free,
a faith that isn't bound
by what we know or what we see.

A faith that trusts the sunshine
even when there is no light,
a faith that hears the morning song's
soft echo in the night.

A faith that somehow rises
past unhappiness or pain,
knowing that in every loss
your goodness will remain.

A faith that finds
your steadfast love
sufficient for all things,
a faith that lifts the heart above
and gives the spirit wings.

When You're Lonely

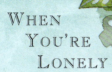

When you're lonely,
I wish you love.

When you're down,
I wish you joy.

When you're troubled,
I wish you peace.

When things are complicated,
I wish you simple beauty.

When things look empty,
I wish you hope.

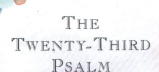

The Twenty-Third Psalm

The Lord is my shepherd,
I shall not want.

He makes me lie down
in green pastures.
He leads me beside still waters;
he restores my soul.

He guides me in
paths of righteousness
for his name's sake.

Even though I walk
through the valley
of the shadow of death,

I fear no evil;
for you are with me;
your rod and
your staff comfort me.

You prepare a table before me
in the presence of my enemies.
You anoint my head with oil.
My cup overflows.

Surely goodness and love
shall follow me
all the days of my life.
And I shall live
in the house of the Lord
for ever.

A Prayer for Those Who Live Alone

Now I'm alone, dear Lord,
stay by my side;
in all my daily needs
be thou my guide.
Grant me good health,
for that indeed I pray,
to carry on my work
from day to day.

Keep pure my mind, my thoughts,
my every deed, let me be kind,
unselfish, in my neighbour's need.
Spare me from fire, from flood,

malicious tongues,
from thieves,
from fear,
and evil ones.

If sickness or an accident befall,
then humbly, Lord, I pray,
hear thou my call.
And when I'm feeling low,
or in despair,
lift up my heart
and help me in my prayer.

I live alone, dear Lord,
yet have no fear,
because I feel your presence
ever near.

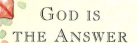

God is the Answer

He comes as a Companion
to the lonely,
a Faithful Friend
who cares and understands.
He comes as a Physician
to the hurting,
with tenderness
and healing in his hands.

He comes as a Protector
to the helpless,
a Shepherd who calls
all his lambs by name,

a Father who sees
every child as special,
whose gentle heart
loves each of us the same.

He comes, the Consolation
of the suffering,
the Light that breaks
through darkness and despair.
He comes, and we discover
that his presence
is the loving answer to
our every prayer.

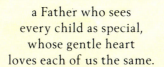

From the Lord of Love

My beloved,
these moments of sadness
are ones that I share with you.
My heart aches as yours.
How I long for you to know
the depth of my love for you
at this time.
It is never easy to lose
that which is precious to you.

It is not easy to say goodbye
before one is ready.

Let me ease
these moments
and comfort you.
I long to touch you
with the peace of my love.
Rest your weariness in me,
for I long to bear
this burden for you.
Come, draw near to me.
Your heavenly Father.

BEYOND THE SHADOWS

Let me look beyond the gathering
shadows of today, Lord.
Help me see tomorrow's hope,
even through my tears.
Shine your gentle sunlight
on the winter of my soul, Lord.
Warm my spirit with your love
until spring reappears.

Since we have been justified
through faith,
we have peace with God
through our Lord Jesus Christ,
through whom we have
gained access
by faith into this grace
in which we now stand.
And we rejoice in the hope
of the glory of God.

ROMANS 5:1-2

You Are There

In this
long night
of my faith, Lord,
sorrow seems
to have no end.
Yet I know the warmth
and comfort
of a never failing friend.

So I rest, securely sheltered
in your love
and gentle care,
knowing even
in the darkness
there is light.
For you are there.

God Has Not Promised

God has not
promised
sun without rain,
joy without sorrow,
peace without pain.
But God has promised
strength for the day,
rest for the labour,
light for the way,
grace for the trials,
help from above,
unfailing sympathy,
undying love.

DEEP PEACE

Deep peace
of the Running Wave
to you.

Deep peace
of the Flowing Air
to you.

Deep peace
of the Quiet Earth
to you.

Deep peace
of the Shining Stars
to you.

Deep peace
of the Son of Peace
to you.

Keep me safe, O God,
for in you I take refuge.
I said to the Lord,
'You are my Lord;
apart from you
I have no good thing.'

PSALMS 16:1-2

Change

Things change.
People change.
My life's changed.
It will change more,
in small ways,
and in big ways.
Nothing's certain;
what shall I build my life on?

I built it around a person;
thought it was secure.
Things change.
People change.
Life changes.
God doesn't.

Michael Forster

True Contentment

I have learned to be content whatever the circumstances. I know what it is to be in need, and I know what it is to have plenty. I have learned the secret of being content in any and every situation, whether well fed or hungry, whether living in plenty or in want. I can do everything through Christ who gives me strength.

PHILIPPIANS 4:11-13

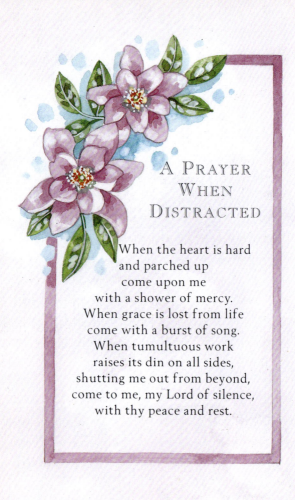

A Prayer When Distracted

When the heart is hard
and parched up
come upon me
with a shower of mercy.
When grace is lost from life
come with a burst of song.
When tumultuous work
raises its din on all sides,
shutting me out from beyond,
come to me, my Lord of silence,
with thy peace and rest.

When my beggarly heart
    sits crouched,
  shut up in a corner,
  break open the door
and come with the ceremony
    of a king.
When desire blinds the mind
  with delusion and dust,
    O thou holy one,
    thou wakeful,
  come with thy light
   and thy thunder.

My God, my God,
why have you forsaken me?
Why are you so far from saving me,
so far from the words
of my groaning?
O my God, I cry out by day,
but you do not answer,
by night, and am not silent.
Yet you are enthroned
as the Holy One;
you are the praise of Israel.
In you our fathers put their trust;
they trusted
and you delivered them.
They cried to you
and were saved;
in you they trusted
and were not disappointed.

Psalm 22:1-5

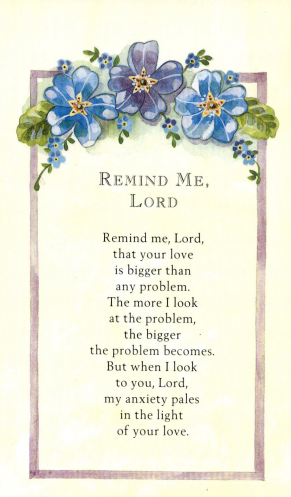

REMIND ME, LORD

Remind me, Lord,
that your love
is bigger than
any problem.
The more I look
at the problem,
the bigger
the problem becomes.
But when I look
to you, Lord,
my anxiety pales
in the light
of your love.

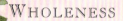

WHOLENESS

God,
you made me;
I'm your creation.
You knew me
from the womb,
even before;
I'm your creation.

They say I need a partner,
a spouse
an 'other half'.

You made me:
did you make me inadequately?
I'm your creation:
did you miss something?

I need friends,
I need people,
everyone does.
But I can be whole.
Without an 'other half'.

You made me:
I'm your creation;
I am complete
in you.

MICHAEL FORSTER

I am convinced
that neither death
nor life,
neither angels
nor demons,
neither the present
nor the future,
nor any powers,
neither height
nor depth,
nor anything else
in all creation,
will be able to
separate us
from the love of God
that is in Christ Jesus
our Lord.

ROMANS 8:38-39

Hold My Hand

Hold my hand, Lord.
Walk me through the loneliness
and the valley of my sorrow.
Hold onto me when I'm too afraid
to think about tomorrow.
Let me lean on you, Lord,
when I'm too weary to go on.
Hold my hand, Lord,
through the night
until I see the light of dawn.

The Lord
is a refuge
for the oppressed,
a stronghold
in times of trouble.
Those who know
your name
will trust in you,
for you, Lord,
have never forsaken
those who seek you.

PSALM 9:9-10